THE DAPPY ADVENTURES OF DIPPY DAN

DIPPY AND THE COAT OF MANY COLOURS

Bible stories told rather differently

By Dan Carlton

Preface.

Children in this modern age have been deprived of many things but especially the ability to make good, informed decisions in later life with regard to their spiritual well-being. This series of Dippy Dan Bible stories attempts in part to address this deficiency in the lives of so many children who may for whatever reason be deprived of the great stories of the Bible. By introducing them via our own wonderful Dippy Dan Character who, although amazingly intelligent has the capacity to do the Dippiest things imaginable that get him into all kinds of trouble. We hope and pray that by God's Grace they may grow up to remember these timeless stories and in doing so come to understand something of the loving heart of God for all who will take the time to seek Him.

Mission Statement.

The Author is a retired Christian Missionary who has spent more than forty years ministering to children at home and abroad.

For centuries the great truths of the Bible have been portrayed via art, music, drama and in modern times through movies and internet games etc. So using a cartoon character like Dippy Dan has given us an opportunity to enable children everywhere to identify with Dippy's antics and behaviour. But whilst the adventures of Dippy Dan are naturally fiction and fun, our sincere intention is not to trivialise the main reason for using this cartoon media but to teach children something about the Holy Bible from the wonderful stories therein and in turn let them enjoy Dippy's exciting adventures.

We wish all who come into contact with the adventures of Dippy Dan to be made aware that we believe the stories of the Bible to be true and we desire that children would somehow find out for themselves what these truths mean in this Godless generation.

Were it possible to reach children some other way solely via Church activities then this great work would not be necessary and so we endeavour to provide an additional alternative that is both fun and informative for children and of course for the Glory of God.

The Dappy Adventures of Dippy Dan
First published in Great Britain in 2018 by:

Dippy Dan Books
United Kingdom

Credits:
*Special thanks are given to my wife Anita who has
endured hundreds of hours of my absence, her patience
and loving support has made this work possible.
Grateful thanks too are given to my Daughter Maria
who has diligently edited this book.*

*Thanks also to our Proof-reader Josephine Gabriel.
Find her here: https://vitalwrite.wordpress.com/*

Acknowledgements:

Acknowledgement to Freepik.com for many of the images
illustrated in this book, including Joseph, Sam and Dylan and to
istock.com for our own registered Dippy Dan images.

*Friends and Heroes Productions Limited have kindly
allowed us to use the image on page 43.
We are proud to promote the beautiful, inspirational
children's Bible resources that Friends and Heroes
produce to all our Dippy Dan readers worldwide.*

*Find Friends and Heroes on these two websites below:
www.friendsandheroes.com
www.friendsandheroes.tv*

Contents

INTRODUCTION:

In the first series of Dippy Dan's adventures we read that Dippy had discovered a secret cave on a small deserted island while on holiday and when he went deep inside the cave he found a big green time machine. Dippy entered the time machine and found to his amazement that he was able to travel back in time to some amazing places, to meet some very interesting people! Join Dippy Dan again on this, his second adventure.

Chapter One

Summer holidays are Dippy Dan's favourite because it means that he can spend lots of time having fun.

Now it's summer, it's time for the real adventure to start, thought Dippy with a smile.

For Dippy Dan and his family, it was a very special day when Dippy's Mum announced that they were going to their Nanny Wendy's farm in Scotland for their summer holiday. It brought a big hooray from Dippy and his twin sisters Poppy and Sue but Dippy's brother Dylan wasn't very happy. Nanny Wendy, affectionately known as grumpy Granny Haggis has a big farm with lots of Cows and chickens. Dylan was chased by the big brown Cow the last time they were there.

Dippy knew that it would be an ideal place for him to take his big green time machine where no one would see it because there were lots of barns, stables, as well as a big old corrugated tin Cow shed with big friendly black and white Cows wandering around. But the problem was getting it there.

Dippy sat inside his time machine and wondered if there was a way of getting his time machine to go wherever he wanted, without needing to take it himself; a bit like he'd seen on the television, where people and things could be beamed from one place to another. So Dippy went to visit his Uncle Sid, who he knew was a mad Scientist and an amazing Inventor and who lived just along the lane with his Auntie Maisy.

"Hi Uncle Sid," said Dippy, as he walked into his Uncle's workshop which was hidden away at the bottom of the garden, where his Uncle Sid spent hours inventing strange and wonderful things.

"Well, hello young Dippy, how you are getting on?" he said. Dippy thought for a moment.

"I'm alright Uncle, thank you. You know that programme on the tele Uncle, you know, the one about the Police box time machine?"

"You mean Doctor Who?"

"That's the one," replied Dippy. "Well...er, I have a time machine too, but I have a problem and I think you can help me Uncle Sid?"

"Are you really asking me to believe that you have a time machine Dippy?"

"Yes Uncle, and if you come home with me to my Dippy cave, you can see it for yourself."

When Dippy's uncle arrived inside Dippy's time machine hanger (Dippy Cave) he just stood there in amazement.

"What?" declared Uncle Sid, "What the heck is that?" and stood there with his hands on his hips.

"It's my big green time machine," said Dippy and then began to wonder if he had made a mistake by asking his Uncle Sid to help him.

"Erm... I need you to help me to do something important. Here, let me open the door and show you," said Dippy, pulling open the big green door.

After examining Dippy's time machine, Uncle Sid came back out.

"Exactly what is it you want me do for you Dippy?"

"I need a special kind of remote control, that will make my time machine go wherever I need it to be, otherwise I have to take it with me and bring it back again." Dippy thought it was a good opportunity to also ask his Uncle Sid for something else.

"When I found my time machine, inside it I found a microphone gizmo which helped me to speak to different people in different languages, it works okay with this earphone but I think it may need to be plugged into something else too because there is a lead dangling and I don't know what it does." Uncle Sid had a look, raised his eyebrow and said,

"Hmm, neither do I Dippy and besides how do you suppose I am going to be able to do all this?"

"Don't know," replied Dippy, "But you are a Scientist and an Inventor, there must be a way?"

"Right, well it may take some time Dippy my boy, I will see what I can do but I can't make any promises you know." Dippy smiled, confident his Uncle could do anything and said,

"You can do it Uncle Sid; you can do anything!"

Uncle Sid's tool bag was full of strange and interesting things which Dippy had never seen before and after a couple of hours of fumbling around inside the time machine and after a lot of head scratching, Uncle Sid came out.

"Here you are Dippy, said Uncle Sid, "Take this green remote controller, I think you may just be in luck this time." Still amazed by all that he had seen.

"According to my scientific calculations you should be able to call your time machine to come to you wherever you are." Uncle Sid took a deep breath and went on.

"All you need to do now is to plug your language gizmo in and clip that special gold key card of yours onto the back of it and away you go, not bad eh?"

"That's fantastic Uncle Sid," said Dippy, "How did you manage to make the new remote control for my time machine so quickly?" Dippy's Uncle Sid shrugged his shoulders.

"Didn't I tell you I'm a genius?" he said with a big grin on his face and then continued.

"The truth is Dippy, I didn't make it because while I was checking out how your time machine works, I accidentally opened that secret draw there and I found this inside, so I didn't need to make anything.

"Hey you could call it your BGTM remote, you know what I mean Dippy?"

"No not really Uncle," answered Dippy.

"Well B is for Big, G is for Green, T is for Time and M is for Machine."

"Oh I get it Uncle, that's what I'll call it then, my BGTM remote." Uncle Sid smiled and slapped Dippy on the back.

"That's my boy, you got it, shall we try it out then?"

"Sure, let's do it?" said Dippy excitedly. So Uncle Sid showed Dippy how to use his new BGTM remote control and especially the big yellow button which did something truly fantastic.

"Press that big yellow button Dippy," said Uncle Sid and so Dippy pressed it and his BGTM remote control shrank to the size of a small matchbox.

"Wow Uncle, that's just amazing," said Dippy in astonishment.

"Now let's see, we'll send it to my workshop and then we can go and see if it gets there, okay?"

So after setting the date and time and speaking into the speaker to tell his time machine where to go, Dippy pressed the red control button and his time machine just vanished into thin air.

"Incredible," said Uncle Sid, "let's go and find it."

They both walked back to Uncle Sid's workshop and there standing in the middle of his workshop was Dippy Dan's big green time machine.

"Wow that really is amazing," said Dippy.

"Thank you, shall I send it back to my Dippy cave again?" Uncle Sid replied, "Of course Dippy but promise me that one day you will take me somewhere special in your time machine, perhaps to meet one of my heroes from the past?"

"Sure Uncle, will do!" said Dippy as his time machine vanished again and off ran Dippy back to his Dippy cave, happy and excited. Dippy clipped his gold key card for his time machine onto the back of his new

BGTM remote controller and pressed the big yellow button and popped it into his pocket.

"Come on everyone we need to get going," said Dippy's Dad, slamming the boot of the car down.

"Everybody ready for a wonderful holiday then?"

"Yay, it's going to be great," shouted Poppy.

Dippy was too busy playing with his new BGTM remote controller and then lifted up his head as though he was lost in another world!

"Yeah, I'm ready Dad." A couple of days later Dippy and his family were up at Nanny Wendy's farm way up in the Highlands of Scotland.

"Hello everyone, welcome to Scotland," shouted Granny Haggis in her broad Scottish accent.

"Hiya Nanny," said Dippy smiling broadly and after lots of hugs they all went inside the farm cottage, to find a table laid out with lots of goodies that Nanny Wendy had prepared for them all.

After lunch, Dippy went up into the Cow shed loft and began to set up his BGTM remote and in a flash, his time machine appeared right before his eyes.

He went inside and just sat there day-dreaming of all the wonderful places he could go to and imagined all the things he could do for people from thousands of years in the past.

That night Dippy Dan went to bed and sat up thinking where he was going to go next. He got out his blue Bible to look at all the wonderful stories.

Dippy flicked through the pages and saw all the stories that he loved. There was Moses and his brother Aaron and there were great prophets like Elijah and Jeremiah and King Solomon but then Dippy's eyes fell upon the story of Joseph and his coat of many colours and he lay there imagining how amazing it would be to visit Joseph in his big green time machine and see his beautiful coat and visit Egypt, even see Pharaoh too maybe.

Dippy's Mum would tell him a story every night but sometimes his Dad would too and make laugh.

His brain was working overtime as usual and then it came to him in a flash!

Got it! said Dippy, almost out loud. I will go to see Joseph and he can show me his coat of many colours.

Suddenly Dippy could hear his Mummy's footsteps coming up the stairs; she was bringing him a cup of hot chocolate and he knew that she would read to him one of his favourite stories, from his little blue Bible.

"Are you all tucked in Dippy?" she asked and sat down on the edge of his bed.

"Now tell me what Bible story you would like me to read to you Dippy?" asked his Mum.

"Let me think," said Dippy, "Oh I know" he mumbled," as if he had only just thought of which one he wanted. (Can you guess which one he chose?)

"I would like you to read Joseph and his coat of many colours please Mum? that story is just amazing."

Dippy continued with a cheeky grin,

"And tomorrow I think I will go and visit him in my time machine." His Mummy smiled and said,

"Of course Dippy," she said shaking her head and smiling at her amazing little Time Traveller.

"But you had better make sure you are back in time for breakfast? or Dylan will eat all the bacon!"

And so Dippy Dan's Mummy began to read Dippy the wonderful story of Joseph and his coat of many colours from Dippy's own little blue Bible.

Dippy Dan's Mummy tells Dippy the story of Joseph and the coat of many colours, and boy what a story it is too.
Just imagine being able to go back in time to meet wonderful people like Joseph.

Chapter Two

The Bible story below of Joseph and all that happened to him is taken from Genesis chapter 37.

This is the story about a young man named Joseph. His father's name was Jacob and they lived in Canaan, where his grandfather was from. Joseph was seventeen. He had eleven brothers, only one was younger than him, called Benjamin. Can you imagine having eleven brothers to play with… or fight with?

Because Joseph was one of the youngest sons, his father spent more time with him and he became very special to him. So, Jacob had a special coat made for Joseph. They didn't have coats like us back then, so this was a very special coat. It was very beautiful and had every colour you could imagine in it.

All of Joseph's older brothers saw this and they got very jealous. The word jealous means that Joseph's brothers disliked him because they thought his father liked him more because he got the special coat. They got so jealous they couldn't even say a kind word to him. One day Joseph had a dream and he went to go and tell his brothers.

"Guess what?" he said. "Last night I had a strange dream. We were tying up bunches of grain out in the field when suddenly my bunch stood up, while all of yours gathered around and bowed to me."

The brothers looked at each other in disgust, but Joseph continued. "Then I had another dream that the sun, moon, and eleven stars bowed down to me."

"Who do you think you are?" The brothers said.

"Do you think that you are better than all of us? Do you think that we would ever bow down to you?" This made the brothers dislike Joseph even more.

When he told his father about his dreams he said they were strange but thought carefully about what Joseph had told him.

A few days later Joseph's father asked him to check on his brothers. They were in the fields quite a distance away so Joseph went out to find them. When the brothers saw Joseph in the distance, they made a plan to kill him. But when Reuben, Joseph's oldest brother heard this he said,

"Let's not kill him, just throw him in a well out here in the field." He said this because he was secretly planning to come back and rescue Joseph when the other brothers had left.

So when Joseph came to them, they took off his beautiful coat of many colours and they threw him in an empty well. A little while later a group of merchants came by, who were going to sell some things in Egypt. One of the brothers spoke up,

"Why don't we sell him to those people, that way we never have to see him again and we don't have to kill him."

The other brothers liked this idea, so they sold him to the people who were going to Egypt. Unfortunately, Reuben had been working and hadn't seen what happened so when he returned to the well, Joseph was gone. He had been sold to an important man named Potiphar, an assistant to the Pharaoh of Egypt.

The rest of the brothers took Joseph's beautiful coat and dipped it in animal blood and took it back to their father. When the father saw this he cried:

"Some animal has killed my son." He cried for many days, so much that nobody could comfort him.

Now Joseph had started out as a slave, but the Lord was with Joseph and he helped him do everything right. So Potiphar made him his helper and put him in charge of everything that he owned. The problem came when Potiphar's wife lied about Joseph to her husband, so Potiphar had Joseph put into jail.

The Lord was still with Joseph in jail and the warden put Joseph in charge of all the prisoners. He never worried because the Lord was with him and helped him do everything right.

After Joseph had been in jail for some time, a cupbearer and a baker to Pharaoh was sent there. One night each of them had a dream. They told their dreams to Joseph and he told the cupbearer that he would soon be let out of jail.

"Please tell Pharaoh about me, and ask him to get me out of here," Joseph said,

When the cupbearer was freed he forgot about what Joseph did. So Joseph stayed in jail for two more years. Until one day the Pharaoh had a dream that nobody could explain to him. The cupbearer then remembered what Joseph had done for him and Joseph was brought to Pharaoh.

"Can you understand dreams?" Pharaoh asked.

"I can't, but God helps me," Joseph replied. After Pharaoh had told him his dream Joseph explained: "God is warning you. There will be seven years when nothing will grow and there won't be any food for anyone."

"What can I do?" Pharaoh asked.

"God has shown you what to do. There will be seven years before the bad years that will be very good. So good, that there will be extra food for everyone. If you save a little bit of each year's harvest you will have enough to get you through the bad years," said Joseph.

Pharaoh believed all that Joseph told him and put him in charge of all the land of Egypt. People came from all countries to buy grain from Joseph, because the whole world was in need of food. Some of those people were Joseph's brothers. When his brothers came, Joseph recognised them, but they did not know who he was. It had been over 10 years since they had seen him.

The brothers all bowed to him because he was an important person. Just as he dreamed they would at the beginning.

After a few meetings with his brothers, Joseph accused them of spying, threw them in the dungeon and only offered to let them go if they would go back home to Canaan and bring Benjamin to him. They agreed, but Joseph kept one of his brothers in the dungeon, so that they would do what he asked of them.

So Benjamin was brought to Joseph and Joseph could not keep his secret any longer and said to his brothers.

"I am Joseph! Is my father alive?" But his brothers couldn't answer him because they were afraid. Then Joseph said,

"Come here. I am your brother, the one you sold. Do not worry and do not be angry at yourselves for selling me because God has put me here to save the people from starving."

His father, his brothers, and their families came to live in Egypt with Joseph. They had all the food they needed.

End of Bible story.

———————

When she had finished reading, Dippy Dan's Mummy closed the Bible and said,

"Now you get some sleep young man, you have a long journey tomorrow in your time machine."

"Oh Muum, I know you don't believe me," answered Dippy and kissed his Mummy goodnight, rolled over and fell fast asleep, dreaming of his next adventure.

An explorer always wants to go exploring but Dippy Dan is a rather unusual explorer and he's in a hurry to get away in his big green time machine but gets held up. How will Dippy get away?

Chapter Three

The morning couldn't come quick enough for Dippy. He ate his breakfast in a hurry.

"Slow down Dippy, you will get a tummy upset if you

eat so quickly," said his Mummy.

"Why are you in such a crazy rush this morning?" she asked.

Dippy looked up from his breakfast bowl with his mouth full and mumbled,

"Oh, sorry Mum, I'm just excited at going up to the old Quarry to look for fossils of Dinosaurs. I read that there are lots of fossils and bones up there.

"Well I hope the Dinosaur doesn't have you for his dinner Dippy," said his Daddy and everyone laughed but Dippy was too busy finishing his breakfast to laugh.

"And make sure you stay well away from any machinery, best to stay close to the road, it's dangerous down there you know?"

"Sure Dad," he said with his mouth still full of food.

"Catch you later then," shouted Dippy as he ran out the front door, while Dippy's Mummy just stood there in the doorway shaking her head and smiling.
So Dippy headed towards the Cow in the yard.

As he arrived at the Cow shed, his brother Dylan was there waiting for him with Zip the dog.

"Can I come to the Quarry with you Dippy, cos I want to find some Dinosaur fossils and bones too?"

Dippy couldn't think of any way of getting away from Dylan and back up to the Cow shed loft, to use his BGTM remote. Dippy Dan had to take Dylan's mind off going to the Quarry with him, so he came up with an idea. Dippy loved his brother Dylan. And said,

"Any other time but not today Dylan, besides it looks like it's going to rain."

Dylan didn't look too happy with his brother's answer so Dippy Dan continued and said,

"Look Dylan, what we need is a list of all the Dinosaurs so that we can go and find fossils and know what each one is called. Nanny Wendy has lots of books on different Dinosaurs and I want you to go indoors and ask Nanny to write down all the names of different Dinosaurs and then we can go up the Quarry and find their fossils, okay?" Dylan looked suspiciously at his brother and replied,

"Ok, I guess so but then we can go get some fossils, yeah?" he said smiling at Dippy.

"Sure Dylan, off you go then, I'll catch you later."

So off ran Dylan to get his list of Dinosaurs while Dippy crept up to the Cow shed loft, without anyone seeing him. Right then, thought Dippy,

I'll get my BGTM remote, and there, that's made it bigger. Clever old Uncle Sid finding out that I can shrink it so that it just slips into my pocket. Dippy made a few adjustments and there, as if by magic, his big green time machine appeared in front of him.

Good thing I was able to smuggle out this packet of biscuits he mumbled and I've got my football too.

Dippy prepares his time machine to travel way back into the past and makes friends with someone who doesn't realise just how naughty he is!

Chapter Four

Dippy Dan opened the big green door and sat inside his time machine. He began to adjust the time and pressed a few coloured buttons and... whoosh, he was gone. A few moments later he felt his time machine land somewhere, but where?

Just hope it's somewhere close to where Joseph lives mumbled Dippy under his breath.

Dippy shrank his BGTM remote and pushed it into his pocket and prepared to go on another adventure and one that he would never forget!

When Dippy opened the door of his time machine he found himself inside what looked like an old derelict Palace and there in front of him stood a little boy.

"Who are. you, how did you get in here?" he said with a gasp. Dippy didn't know how to explain.

"Hello, my name is Dippy Dan and I have come from the future to make friends with you, what is your name?" he asked. The little boy looked frightened.

"My name is Samuel, and I live in the village." Samuel came closer and looked inside Dippy's time machine with his mouth wide open in amazement.

"Did you bring this in through the window?" Dippy laughed, knowing he would not be believed.

"I will tell you later, please can I call you Sam?" asked the strange little Time Traveller.

"I suppose that would be alright," said the boy; as they both stood there smiling at one another.

"Do you know someone called Joseph?" asked Dippy. "He's my neighbour," answered Sam. "Hey what is that?" "It's a football." said Dippy. "Here, let me show you what you do with it, it's fun to play with, we can have a kick about."

Dippy brought his football out from inside his time machine to show Sam and before long they were kicking the football up and down the Palace floor.

Sam was overjoyed to have a friend because he spent many lonely days wandering around on his own, but he was about to be in very big trouble!

Around the Palace were cottages where women left food to cool off on window ledges.

In one cottage window they saw a lovely big cake, much too tempting to pass by; so Dippy lifted himself up as high as he could to reach the cake, grabbed a big slice of it and ran back into the derelict Palace, to eat it with his new friend Sam.

They grinned at each other for getting away with having been so naughty. Suddenly they heard shouting outside. Someone had seen them and told Mama Kish that two naughty boys have ran off with a piece of her cake!

"Oh no," whispered Sam. "It's Mama Kish. It was her cottage that we took the slice of cake from."

Dinosaurs don't scare Dippy, and when he goes off with his new friend and his brother Dylan to hunt for fossils, he gets them into big trouble!

Chapter Five

Dippy could think of only one way to escape. He grabbed Sam's arm and opened the door to his time machine.

"Right Sam, you stand there, this will only take a few seconds." He slammed the door shut, then… whoosh, they disappeared through space and time and when Mama Kish went into the old derelict Palace, the two naughty little boys that stole some of her cake were nowhere to be seen.

When Dippy's time machine stopped, Samual wondered where they were, but Dippy knew exactly, because he had set his time machine clock to go back to the Cow shed loft at his Nanny Wendy's farm.

"Right, you stay here Sam and I will get you some clothes to change into otherwise Granny Haggis will wonder where you have come from." So Dippy left Sam up in the Cow shed loft while he went off to get some clothes. When Dippy Dan entered the farm house, his Mum said,

"Well, it's nice to see you young man, did you find any dinosaur fossils?" Dippy whistled as he went past his Mum, pretending that he hadn't heard her.

"Fossils? oh them, er, well sort of I guess, I've just got to get something Mum." Dippy's Mum threw her hands in the air and said,

"Boys, what can you do with them?" and smiled at Granny Haggis, who was sitting in her rocking chair, knitting Dippy a woolly cardigan.

When Dippy came back up to the Cow shed loft, he emptied his camping rucksack onto the floor.

"Here Sam, try some of these clothes on, I think they'll fit alright." So, Sam got dressed up in some of Dippy's old clothes.

"You look a bit odd," said Dippy.

"But you'll do I reckon. Just let me do all the talking when we get indoors, and everything will go just fine."

Dippy was so happy to have a friend and quickly took Sam into his house to introduce him to his Mum and Granny Haggis, who opened the Cookie jar and handed Sam a big almond Cookie with chocolate on top.

"Where did you say you came from Sam?" asked Dippy's Dad.

"He's from another Country far away," replied Dippy quickly. "Actually Dad, he got here in my time machine if you really want to know!" Dippy hoped that his Dad wouldn't ask any more questions.

"Oh, I see," answered Dippy's Dad. "You mean the time machine that took you back to the Stone Age, right?" Dippy shrugged his shoulders and smiled.

"Of course Dad, how else do you think he got here?" Everyone laughed and sat down together at Granny Haggis' big long dining table, to have lunch.

Dippy's family giggled at seeing Sam use his knife and fork and the faces he pulled as he ate his sausage and chips. Sam smiled back at them because he knew that they weren't really laughing at him. He couldn't tell them he came from a time thousands of years in the past, from a place that had food which they would never have seen. Dylan put his knife and fork down and asked his brother Dippy,

"Can we go to the Quarry now please? You said we could if I got a list of dinosaur fossils out of Nanny's book." Sam looked confused.

"Ok, Dylan we will go to the Quarry for a while before Sam has to go back home but you must promise to stay with us all the time because Dad said it is very dangerous up there and we can only stay near the road, okay?" Dylan was excited and agreed.

"Ok, that sounds like a plan," he said, so off they went to the Quarry.

As the boys wandered off down the road towards the Quarry, Dippy looked at his new friend Sam and felt so sad, that soon he would have let him go back home to his world far away, to another time where the two of them would never be able to have any more fun or get into trouble together! So Dippy decided to make the most of the last day that he and Sam were having together.

And wanting to have some mischievous fun, Dippy ran off and hid behind the big trees that lined the long lane, that lead down to the Quarry.

"Come and find me?" shouted Dippy. Dylan and Sam ran round and round the trees searching for him and suddenly Dippy jumped out from behind a tree and said in a strange, loud voice,

"Here I am, you didn't catch me, so I win!"

Dippy knew that he would be in big trouble if anything went wrong and that his Mum and Dad wouldn't ever trust him again if Dylan got hurt in any way so he stayed on the road as his Dad had told him to and had really intended to stay away from the Quarry lake and massive piles of sand! But Dippy's good intentions soon changed and Dippy began being naughty again, even after he promised his Daddy, he'd be good boy!

All three boys arrived at the Quarry and began searching for Dinosaur fossils but found nothing, and bit by bit they drew nearer and nearer to where Dippy's Dad had told them they were not to go!

"Didn't Daddy say that we shouldn't leave the road Dippy?" asked Dylan.

"Well, we won't find anything up here. If we are careful, we can go a bit closer, just stay close to me and we'll be fine," answered Dippy.

They hunted everywhere for fossils, but they didn't find anything and soon decided to forget the fossils and play in the big piles of sand instead, chasing each other around and just having fun, throwing sand everywhere.

Suddenly a man climbed down from one of the cranes and shouted,

"Hey, you boys, clear off, this is private property."

So, with no fossils and no more fun to be had the boys left the Quarry, with the man still shaking his fist at them in the distance.

"Dad is going to go mad when he finds out what we've done," moaned Dylan, Dippy answered,

"If we are lucky, he won't know and we can forget all about it, "But I bet Mummy will find out, replied Dylan, "She always does!"

Dippy and Sam were about to face the music for stealing the big slice of cake and that was just the start of their problems because Mama Kish had been to Sam's house to tell his Dad! Oops.

Chapter Six

The three boys wandered back home again. It was fun while it lasted and at least Dylan got to go to the Quarry after all. So, after Sam had said goodbye to everyone, both boys strolled back to the Cow shed and with no one watching, they both climbed up into the loft.

Dippy's BGTM took only a few seconds to return to the derelict Palace and out they went back to Sam's house. As they passed the cottage where they had stolen the slice of cake, there stood Mama Kish!

"You naughty boys, I know what you have done. I have been to tell your Father young Samuel and he is waiting for you." Sam blamed Dippy of course!

When they got to Sam's house, there was no one at home, so Sam knocked on next door and there sat Jacob.

Joseph's Dad Jacob was old and grey, and he loved Sam and had always believed he was an honest boy.

"This is my new friend Dippy Dan," said Sam. Jacob looked up and said,

"Hmm, yes I know, I have had a visit from Mama Kish, she is very angry with you both and so is your Dad, why did you do this to one of our oldest neighbours?"

"I'm sorry Sir, we only took one slice, it was such a nice cake, but I am so very sorry," said Sam. Dippy bowed his head in shame.

"So am I Sir," said Dippy. Jacob looked at them both and the angry frown on his face turned to a warm smile.

"I forgive you both and after your Dad has punished you Samuel, I want you to run some errands for Mama Kish, to make up for the wrong you have done." Sam agreed to do whatever Mama Kish wanted him to do.

Mama Kish was greatly loved by everyone in the village and especially by Jacob who was very sad to see this happen but glad that the boys were sorry for what they had done.

When the boys both knew that everything was alright again and that they had been forgiven, they went into the kitchen and Jacob got some bread and fig jam for Dippy and Sam to eat.

They sat there munching away naughtily grinning at each other.

In came Joseph's son Joeph, he lifted up his arms in confusion and stared at Dippy Dan because he had never seen such a strange looking boy in all of Canaan and then asked,

"Who are you boy, what are you doing here?"

"My name is Dippy Dan, I hope you don't mind me being here?" Jacob smiled at his son Joseph.

"It's alright Joseph. Dippy is Samuel, our next-door neighbour's new friend, please make him welcome?" So, Joseph sat down with Sam and Dippy to share the bread and fig jam with them.

Dippy felt such love from him and they chatted away like they had known each other for years.

Jacob turned to Joseph and spoke very quietly to him and said,

"Son, will you go down to your brothers later and take the food I prepared for them?"

"Sure Dad," answered Joseph winking at Dippy.

"I'll go as soon as I have seen Sam's friend back home safely," and then lovingly patted Sam on the head. Joseph loved Sam and always wanted a little brother of his own.

"Come on Sam, let us take your friend Dippy Dan back home to his Mummy and Daddy." Dippy had to go but he wasn't planning to go home!

The boys all smiled at each other as they left Jacob.

Dippy couldn't look at Joseph because he knew what would soon happen to him and he knew too that he wouldn't be able to do anything to change things, even though he knew the Bible said it would all go wrong, the moment he left!

To make sure that Joseph would take them to the old Palace, he said to Sam with a knowing nod,

"Sam? I've got something to show you before I go."

After a lot of explaining, Sam took his next-door neighbour Joseph and Dippy Dan back up to the old derelict Palace, with Joseph looking a bit confused and slightly worried because he knew that the boys were up to something!

Dippy reached into his pocket and took out his BGTM remote and pushed the big yellow button. The two brother's eyes widened with amazement and then after making a few adjustments, there in front of them all appeared Dippy's big green time machine.

Dippy opened the door and Joseph grabbed Sam to protect him from what he thought was a horrible green monster, but Sam told him that everything was okay and that it was going to take Dippy back home. Joseph let Sam go and they all hugged each other.

It was time for Dippy to go and with a heavy heart Dippy sat down inside his time machine. He felt very sad to leave these wonderful friends behind.

Dippy Dan must go but he takes his BGTM forward in time to find out more about Joseph, but nothing could prepare him for what happens next!

Chapter Seven

"Bye Sam, bye Joseph, see you again soon," shouted Dippy and closed the door leaving his two wonderful friends looking up in amazement and waving, as his time machine zoomed off into space.

Dippy felt such great love for his two new friends, especially Sam, who he knew he would miss.

The adventure isn't over yet, mumbled Dippy to himself, because he knew that he had one last place to go before he was able to go home.

"We're off to Egypt then," he whispered.

Dippy had decided to visit Joseph at the other end of his journey. He remembered that the Bible said, that Joseph was thrown into a big hole in the ground by his jealous older brothers and Dippy wanted to hear Joseph tell the story in his own words, just like Daniel and Jonah had.

Moments later, Dippy Dan arrived inside Pharaoh's Royal Palace. He had travelled forward in his BGTM many years, to a time when Joseph had become a Prince in the house of Pharaoh, like the Bible says.

Looks like I've landed in an old dungeon inside the Royal Palace, thought a sleepy Dippy and decided not to send his BGTM back to his Dippy cave.

Can't see anyone around, so I better go and see if can find Joseph, he won't remember me I don't suppose. So Dippy went to search for Joseph and when he got to the top of the stairs he heard the sound of Soldier's footsteps marching down the corridor and Dippy hid behind a wall until they had passed and then opened a door.

There outside in the courtyard right in front of him was a Royal Chariot with two big horses. Dippy wondered what it would be like to climb up into it, so up he went and pretended to be the chariot driver.

"Gee-up horsey!" he shouted, and to his surprise and shock, the horses ran off, with Dippy Dan holding on for his life. Without him noticing, Dippy's BGTM remote slipped out of his pocket as the horses raced away into the desert and fell onto the floor of the Chariot.

When the Guards caught up with him and stopped the horses, Dippy was badly shaken up.

"Come with us," they demanded. So Dippy was taken back to the Royal Palace.

"We caught this boy racing off in one of the Royal Chariots my Lord." Dippy looked up and there sitting on his throne was Pharaoh, the ruler of all Egypt.

Pharaoh pulled Dippy's chair closer to him and said,

"Is this true boy?" Dippy didn't know what to say but then pointed his finger at the mighty Pharaoh and said to him in an angry voice,

"It's your silly horses fault for running away." But Joseph nudged him gently and Dippy quickly said,

"Yes Sir," and began to cry. The mighty Pharaoh came down off his seat and bowed down to Dippy and looking into his face with such love, he whispered,

"Don't be afraid, you have done a great wrong to take one of my royal chariots without permission but I will not punish you my son, instead I will hand you over to Joseph here, who is my royal servant."

Dippy stopped crying and felt happier knowing his friend Joseph was there too, to help him and who had become a Prince and a Ruler over all of Egypt.

So the Pharaoh handed Dippy over to Joseph to be told off. Dippy was glad, especially after his friend Joseph had stopped him from upsetting the Pharaoh, by calling his horses silly and blaming them for running away. Silly ol Dippy! So Joseph took Dippy away.

"It's dark outside now Dippy, you must soon make your long journey back home but first I want you to have something to eat." On the way down to the dungeon, where Dippy's BGTM waited, the two friends passed through the Palace kitchen and Joseph told the chief cook to get Dippy Dan something nice to eat.

"Why have you come here Dippy?" asked Joseph and why would you travel so far back in time?"

"I wanted you to tell me your story yourself, of all that happened after I left?" Even though Dippy knew.

"Well Dippy, I know that you are a very special little boy and my neighbour Sam told me all about the wonderful time he spent with your lovely family." Dippy looked up into Joseph's face and said,

"I took my friend Sam far into the future in my big green time machine. We went to my house for dinner and then afterwards, we went to the Quarry to look for Dinosaur fossils, but the man chased us away, it wasn't fair really, we were only having some fun."

"Never mind," answered Joseph. "There will be another opportunity to find Dinosaur fossils I'm sure.

"Well Dippy," Joseph went on, "Before I tell you my story, I want you to promise me, that you will never do these naughty things again?" Dippy lowered his head in shame and Joseph continued, "My Father told me about Mama Kish and the slice of cake that you and Samuel took and now this dangerous behaviour with one of the Pharaoh's Chariots." Dippy lifted his head and tears rolled down his cheeks and he muttered,

"I'm so sorry Joseph, I'll never do anything like that again." But he knew that he just couldn't promise never to be naughty again for the rest of his life.

Joseph placed his hands on Dippy's head.

"Okay don't cry, I forgive you Dippy, so cheer up and remember that I am your friend and my Dad, Sam and all love you very much."

Then Joseph began to tell Dippy all about what happened to him after he had left Sam and Joseph back in the old derelict Palace.

Dippy gets back to the farm after saying goodbye to his friend and he's in for a big surprise. He won't be able to sweep this one under the carpet!

Chapter Eight

When Joseph had finished speaking to Dippy, he took him by the hand and led him down the stairs to where Dippy Dan's BGTM sat waiting to take him home.

"Remember what you said Dippy, that you would try to be a good boy and God will be watching over you always because he loves you very much too."

The two friends hugged. "Goodbye Dippy, have a safe journey home?" said Joseph with a warm smile.

Joseph waited and waited, expecting Dippy Dan's time machine to zoom off...

...but nothing! It just sat there and didn't go anywhere. Finally, Dippy Dan opened the big green door of his time machine again.

"I've lost my BGTM remote Joseph, I need it to make my time machine work," he said.

"I need to go and find it for you then," replied Joseph. "You must wait here Dippy and I will go and search for it." Dippy told Joseph what it looked like and off went Joseph to search the Royal Chariot where Dippy had dropped his BGTM remote. I hope he finds it, thought Dippy. Then he heard footsteps.

"Got it Dippy," shouted Joseph.

"Phew that was close," replied Dippy and hugged Joseph again before entering his time machine and finally with Joseph waving furiously, Dippy's BGTM zoomed off in a flash and away he went.

When Dippy Dan got back home his Mum called him and said,

"Dippy, a man from the Quarry came to complain that you boys had jumped all over his piles of sand. I told him that I would make sure you were told off and you can go up there in the morning and sweep up the mess you both made."

Dippy took his telling-off like a man which was unusual, because he normally had a moan when his Mummy told him off!

"Sorry Mummy, I will take Dylan up there with me tomorrow morning and tidy up the sand we spread everywhere."

That night Dippy Dan sat up in bed with his arms folded, yawning with exhaustion. His head was spinning as he thought of all the wonderful adventures he had been on. He made up his mind that after going to the Quarry to tidy up, he would go somewhere really exciting again but before he could think of where to go, he was fast asleep.

No one would ever believe that Dippy Dan had been to Canaan and Egypt all in one day and travelled thousands of years back into the past to visit his amazing friends because his time machine was gone for only a few seconds. Dippy found he could set his BGTM to leave for a week and still come back only minutes after it left or even come back before it left, isn't that amazing?

Cleaning up their mess made Dippy realise why they went to the Quarry in the first place, then he has a brainwave which takes him on a very dangerous mission. Does Dylan find out Dippy's secret?

Chapter Nine

The next morning Dippy and Dylan went to the Quarry to clean up the mess they had made, and the Quarry Foreman stood and watched.

"Now you boys," he said, with his fist in the air, "If you ever come back here I won't tell your parents but I will call the police, do you understand?" Dippy and Dylan nodded their heads and finished sweeping up the sand they had got all over the place.

"So glad that's done," said Dippy.

"We still didn't get any Dinosaur fossils or bones though," replied Dylan. Both boys walked back home, tired and fed up. Dippy put arm around his brother.

"It's not your fault Dylan, we just had a bad day!"

When they got home the boy's Mummy was standing there waiting for them.

"What's the matter?" she asked.

"Oh, nothing really, we went and cleaned up the mess and there was a nasty man shouting at us."

"Well," said Dippy's Mum, "That's what you get when you go to places where you are not supposed to be and make a mess everywhere." Dylan sighed and said to his Mum,

"It's all my fault really Mum, I wanted to go up there." Dylan continued, with his eyes looking down at the floor, too ashamed to look up at his Mummy.

"We were only looking for Dinosaur fossils and bones, we weren't doing any harm, honest!"
His Daddy popped his head around the door and said,

"Dinosaurs? Well, you will need to go back in time to the Dinosaur age and get some bones. Maybe Dippy can take you there in his time machine?"

Everyone laughed but that gave Dippy a wonderful idea for a new adventure in his BGTM.

After having a rest and some dinner, Dippy wandered off back to Granny Haggis' Cow shed and within seconds, he was travelling back thousands of years to the time of the Dinosaurs.

Wow, thought Dippy, as he looked out of the window of his BGTM, this must be the Dinosaur era.

All of a sudden Dippy screamed, Oh help! as a big green monster stared into the window at him. I had better get out of here quick and look somewhere else, that's a giant Diplodocus and her baby and if she thinks I have come to take her baby from her, she won't be very happy at all, thought Dippy.

He really wished he could have stayed and have some fun with the lovely baby Diplodocus.

Maybe another time when I've been to other places, he said to himself. As any busy Time-Traveller would!

So Dippy landed close-by. I think I will go and find something and get out of here quickly before I get eaten by one of the Dinosaurs," muttered Dippy.

Then Dippy climbed out of his BGTM and started looking around and lying there on the floor right in front of him were some big old bones of a small Dinosaur.

Dippy was shaking with fear as he picked them up.

Just what I was looking for, he thought and carried them over to his time machine.

I'd better get out of this hot place now and take these Dinosaur bones back home to show Dylan.

Lucky I left the door open, that Dino is far too close for comfort and looks very angry.

So, when Dippy returned to Granny Haggis' Cow shed, he couldn't wait to find Dylan to show him what he had found.

When Dippy got back indoors he put what he'd found onto the kitchen table and imagined what it would have been like to live in the time of Dinosaurs and remembered Fred and Barney Rubble who were his favourites on a programme called the Flintstones.

Wouldn't it be cool to live in a stone house and have a little Dinosaur to clean the house like Fred's wife Wilma does, he thought and quickly spread the bones out on the table so that everyone could see what he had found. They will never believe where I got them, he thought.

"Hey Dylan," shouted Dippy,

"Take a look at these?" Dylan came running in.

"Cor, what are they?" asked Dylan. Dippy didn't really know exactly but wanted to sound like he knew.

"I think it's the bones of a little Diplodocus or something like that." Granny Haggis suddenly appeared, standing outside in the garden and looked in through the window at Dippy and Dylan and saw the old bones on her clean kitchen table.

"You get those out of here young Dippy!" she growled, in a stern and angry voice.

"They look dirty and old, what are they?"

"It's the bones of a little Diplodocus Nanny," said Dylan. But his Nanny wasn't impressed with Dylan's answer.

Nanny Haggis said in her strong Scottish accent,

"Now you boys, you take them back to where you got them from right now." Dippy just smiled at her.

"Don't worry Nanny, they won't hurt anyone, and I can't take them back in any case."

With that he grabbed the rolled up papers of Dinosaurs names that Dylan had found and carried the Dinosaur bones outside into the garden with Dylan and Zip.

Both boys stood outside and examined the strange old bones.

"Did you get them from the Quarry Dippy?"

"No Dylan, I went back thousands of years in my big green time machine, how else do you think I got them?" Dylan shook his head.

"Silly old Dippy, you don't have a big green time machine... do you?"

"Well I might have but if I show you, will you promise not to tell anyone?"

"Yeah I promise, I won't tell anyone." And so Dippy took Dylan by the hand and led him over to the Cow shed but his brother Dylan ran on ahead of him.

"Look Dippy, I'm up here?" shouted Dylan.

"Shh, keep quite Dylan, you'll have everyone know about my time machine by the time you've done."

Dylan said he was sorry and the boys both stood looking at Dippy's big green time machine.

"It's great Dippy, how do you drive it?" Dippy laughed.

"I don't drive it Dylan, it has to be set to a certain time and then I put my gold key-card into this slot."

And to prove he was telling the truth, Dippy took out his BGTM remote controller to show Dylan.

"Cool," muttered Dylan. He couldn't believe his eyes and wanted to go somewhere straight away, maybe to the Ice age, even to outer space!

"Can we go for a ride right now Dippy please, oh please?" Dylan was determined, but Dippy said,

"Not today Dylan but let me think of a wonderful  adventure we can both go on and then you can come with me, okay?"

Dylan looked disappointed but he agreed and both boys went back out and into the farmhouse to settle down for the evening.

"Remember Dylan, that you must never tell anyone about my big green time machine?"

"Alright, you can trust me Dippy, I won't tell anyone... I promise," laughed Dylan! Dippy wasn't very sure that his brother would keep his secret but answered,

"I believe you Dylan... of course I believe you!"

And so, with a big yawn Dippy Dan laid his head down on his pillow, wondering what tomorrow would bring.

"Good night Dylan," yawned Dippy.

"Night night Dippy," replied Dylan and they both drifted off into a deep sleep.

THE END

We hope you enjoyed this Dippy Dan adventure.

For further information or to place an order, please contact our Office Administrator below.

Facebook: @DippyDanBooks
Twitter: @DippyDanBooks

Other adventures in this series:

Dippy in the Ark

Dippy and Goliath

Dippy and the Whale

Dippy in the Lion's den

Dippy on the Gospel road

Dippy in the Garden of Eden

Many more Adventures in the Dippy Pipeline

Printed in Great Britain
by Amazon

39653809R00035